HOW TO
LOSE
A GUY IN
10 DAYS

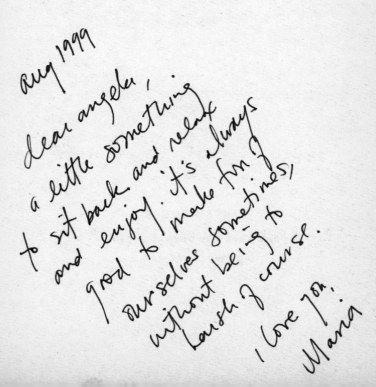

Aug 1999

dear angela,

a little something
to sit back and relax
and enjoy. it's always
good to make fun of
ourselves sometimes,
without being to
laugh of course.

i love you.

Maria

BANTAM BOOKS

New York Toronto London
Sydney Auckland

HOW TO LOSE A GUY IN 10 DAYS

The Universal **DON'TS** of Dating

written by
Michele Alexander & Jeannie Long

created by
Danielle Hoover, Michele Alexander
& Jeannie Long

HOW TO LOSE A GUY IN 10 DAYS

A Bantam Book / October 1998

Library of Congress Cataloging-in-Publication Data

Alexander, Michele.
How to lose a guy in 10 days : the universal don'ts of dating / Michele
Alexander and Jeannie Long.
p.   cm.
ISBN 0-553-38007-9
1. Dating (Social customs)—Humor. 2. Man-woman relationships—Humor.
I. Long, Jeannie. II. Title.
HQ801.A522   1998
646.7'7—dc21   98-18348
CIP
Published simultaneously in the United States and Canada

Bantam Books are published by Bantam Books, a division of Bantam
Doubleday Dell Publishing Group, Inc. Its trademark, consisting of the words
"Bantam Books" and the portrayal of a rooster, is Registered in U.S. Patent
and Trademark Office and in other countries. Marca Registrada. Bantam
Books, 1540 Broadway, New York, New York 10036.

PRINTED IN THE UNITED STATES OF AMERICA

OPM   10 9 8 7 6 5 4 3 2

ACKNOWLEDGMENTS

Jeannie and Michele would like to thank:

Our families: Johnny & Marilyn Long,
Ray & Judy Alexander, Keith & Cassy Alexander,
and Carrie & Shari Lynne Long.

Our friends: Tanya Scheer, David Grant, James
Kirtley, Matt McDowell, Bethany Rogers,
Elizabeth Baker, Sara Pitchford, Heather
Hoffman, Marc Weinbach, Tony George, Ko,
Scott and everyone at Asylm, everyone at
Geffen, and anyone we forgot . . . thanks!

A special thanks to: Jay Mandel, our editor
Katie Hall, Therese McDonald, Kevin James,
Kenneth Norwick, and Ted Volk.

And last but not least—thanks to Brian
Alexander—through which all things were
made possible.

HOW TO
LOSE
A GUY IN
10 DAYS

DAY

1

Meet him at a party.

Ditch your friends
and convince him to
go home with you.

Have sex.

Make sure you let him
know he's not the first.

Do the Helicopter Move.

(Use your imagination.)

After sex, talk.

Ask him if you look fat.

Name his penis.

DAY

2

Break all plans.

Kidnap him.

Don't take him home no matter
how many times he asks.

At breakfast, sit
on the same side as him.

Accuse him of flirting
with the waitress.

Ask him if he thinks she's
prettier than you.

DON'T ORDER ANYTHING.

If he makes you order,
order a small salad with the
dressing on the side.

Ask him if he thinks
you've gotten fat since
you've been dating.

Always make him drive,
even if it's your car.

And sit in the middle.

Swing by Blockbuster
and rent
"When Harry Met Sally."

While watching the movie,
have your roommate come
in and take "candid"
photos of you guys
just "hanging out."

Refer to him as your
boyfriend.

When you drop him off,
FRENCH KISS him.
(The more passionate,
the more memorable.)

Constantly do splits in
front of him to show
him how limber you are.

That night, go out with your
girlfriends and constantly
talk about him.

Analyze everything.

When you get home,
CALL HIM.
(The later the better.)

Beg him to come over.

If you feel it's time,
tell him you love him.

DAY

3

Go over to his house.

Bring him a plant.

Sneak into his room.

While you are there,
grab a sweatshirt and
some boxers.

Put them on immediately.

Take your perfume out
and spray his pillows.
(This allows your scent
to linger.)

Leave an article
of clothing.

If his phone rings,

answer it.

Go hang out in his
roommate's room.

Ask him what the plans
are for that night.

Tell his roommate you
have "several friends you could
set him up with so you guys
can double-date."

(Mention they are
bisexual strippers.)

As soon as you get
home, CALL HIM.

If he doesn't answer,
DO NOT, I repeat DO NOT
leave a message.

This enables you to call back—
again and again.

Call again.

Ask him if he
thought you looked fat
earlier that day.

Call your ugliest friend
for a "Girls' Night Out."
(This will make you
look better.)

Then, show up where he

is supposed to be.

Ask everyone there if
they know him.

Tell them you're dating.

Ask their advice.

Drive by his house—
more than once.

When you get home,
CALL HIM.
(The later, the better.)

Ask him to come over.

If he's too tired, offer
to drive to his house.
If that doesn't work,
bring food.

Before sex, ask him if
he respects you.

Tell him he reminds
you of your dad.

After sex, cry.

DAY

4

Get up early.

Clean his house.

Pump his roommate
for information.

Stay until you are
forced to leave.

Ask him to hang out—
just "you and him"
for once!

Swing by the animal
shelter and pick out
a dog the two of you
should adopt.

Buy him an engraved frame for
the pictures of you and him—
from the day you guys were
just "hanging out."

Leave a copy of "Bride"
magazine and "The Book of
Rules" in a visible area.
(Perhaps the back of the toilet.)

Go see your psychic.

Tell him everything
she says.

If he mentions he doesn't
like one of your friends,
immediately start bagging on
her and tell him you didn't
like her anyway.

Tell him you can't wait for him
to meet your dad, because
they are so much alike.

If he has a sister,
become her best friend.

CALL HIM!

CALL HIM,

again.

Ask him what he's
doing that night.

If he doesn't invite you,
refer to it as
"Boys' Night Out."

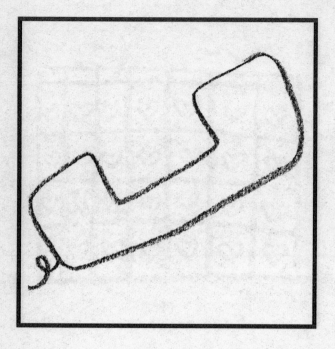

Let him know he can call
later when he gets in.

Wait for his call.

Write your name with
his last name—
over and over again.

When he calls, tell him you
were worried.

But you knew he was going
to call because you have some
sort of psychic connection.

Get dressed.

Drive to his house FAST
before he passes out.

Bring your pillow.

Bring an overnight bag.

Ask him if you can
have a drawer.

Before sex, ask him
if he thinks about you
during the day.

Tell him that you do.

During sex, tell him some
alarming statistic about how
women always marry
someone that reminds
them of their fathers.

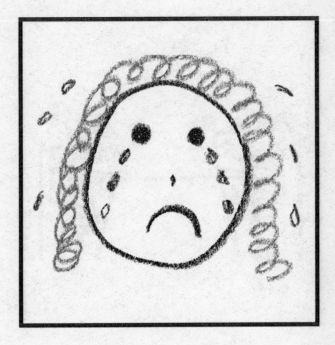

After sex, cry.

Tell him how rich your life
has become since meeting him
and how great it is to finally
be in an adult relationship.

Spoon him.

DAY

5

If you wake up
and he's not there,
DON'T WORRY,
he'll be back.

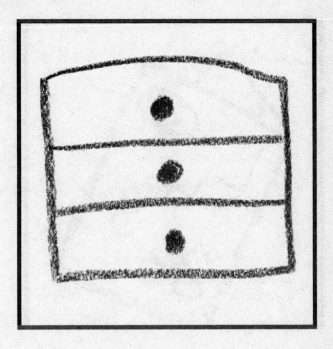

Keep yourself busy.
Go through everything.

Read his old yearbook.

Call his mom and
introduce yourself.

When he comes back,
make sure you are
wearing his shirt,
preferably an oxford.
(Guys love that!)

Start referring to things you read in his yearbook, like . . .

"Remember when you and Scooter got arrested after the football game? That was the funniest story I ever heard."

Ask him if he still has
feelings for Stacy.

If he says he has
to leave to run
errands, ask if you
can tag along.

At the drugstore,
pick up a pregnancy test.

In line, refer to him
as "Daddy."

Talk in your cutest
baby voice—all the time.

Never have any ideas.
Always say,
"Whatever you want."

Find out his favorite bands.

Run out and buy the CDs.

Memorize all the words.

Go out with his friends.

Come back to his house
late-night.

Crawl into bed with him.

Set your mental alarm and
wake up earlier than him and
wrap his arms around you.

DAY

6

Refer back to DAY 1:

"Remember when . . ."

When you call him,
never announce
yourself—from now
on it's "me."

Make him a mix
tape with all "your"
songs on it.

Get your hair cut
like Stacy's.

Have your friends come up to
you and tell you what a cute
couple you make and how
beautiful your children will be.

Buy him an airbrushed
T-shirt with your names
on it and a picture
of his car.

Brag about how
much you DIDN'T eat
that day.

After sex, do the Cosmo
quiz for couples.

DAY

7

Tell him you love him. Immediately ssshhhh him and tell him he doesn't have to say anything, because you know in your heart how he feels.

And besides, your psychic told you so.

Begin making plans for
a romantic getaway.

Join his gym.

Accidentally run into him there.

Anytime you "accidentally"
run into him, call it a weird
"ka-winky-dink."

Always touch him—
even if it's just an elbow.

Talk constantly.

During sex, cry.

After sex, tell him you
stopped taking the pill
because you thought it
was making you fat.

Ask him if he agrees.

DAY

8

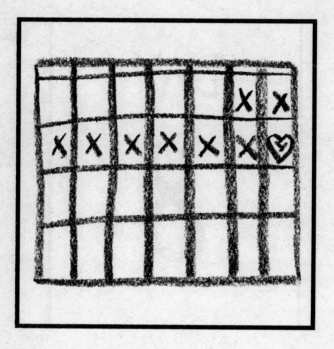

Tell him this is
the longest you've ever
dated someone.

And, that you met
your last boyfriend
on the internet.

Then suggest cybersex.

Suggest abstinence.

Then, next time it will
be more special.

DAY

9

Move into his

neighborhood.

Fly your parents
in to meet him.

Never refer to yourself
in the first person—
from now on it's "we."

Be overly concerned
about the welfare of
"your" plant.

Tell him if it dies, so
does the relationship.

Tell him he's changed
and you don't even
know him anymore.

Suggest couples
therapy.

Constantly ask him
what he's thinking.
Use the phrase "penny
for your thoughts."

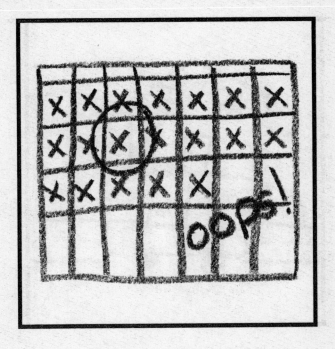

Fake a late period.

(This may give you a
couple extra weeks.)

If you work,
call in sick. (You don't
want to miss him.)

Drive by his house
over and over again.

Leave a poem and
a long-stemmed rose
on his doorstep.

Call his friends,
ask advice.

Hide in his bushes.
(He may be cheating
on you.)

Page him—911.

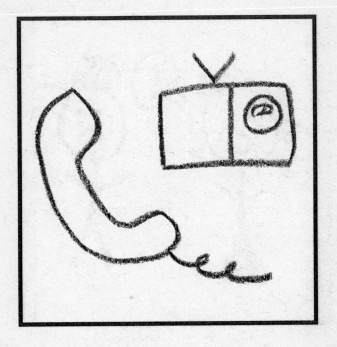

Call Casey Kasem and
request a long-distance
dedication.

Confront him.

Yell, cry, throw your shoe
at him, collapse on the hood
of his car—do anything
to get him back.

If nothing works,
quote the old saying—

"If you love something,
set it free.
If it comes back to you,
it was meant to be."

Go to a party.

Meet someone else.

(And start back at

DAY 1 . . .)

About the writers

Michele and Jeannie grew up
together in Tallahassee, Florida,
and now live in Los Angeles,
California, where they both work
in the music industry. Neither
of them has actually done the
Helicopter Move.